Parenting With a Purpose

BIBLICAL FOUNDATIONS FOR SUCCESSFUL PARENTING

COS DAVIS, ED.D.

CROSS BOOKS

CrossBooks™
1663 Liberty Drive
Bloomington, IN 47403
www.crossbooks.com
Phone: 1-866-879-0502

First published by CrossBooks 10/09/2009

ISBN: 978-1-6150-7056-5 (sc)

Library of Congress Control Number: 2009937729

Printed in the United States of America
Bloomington, Indiana

This book is printed on acid-free paper.

DEDICATION

To my grandchildren: Anna Katherine,
Walker, Alec and Jake; gifts from God

Contents

INTRODUCTION

What is the measure of success as a parent? Many human endeavors show the direct correlation between effort and result. For example, if you follow the blueprint exactly you get the house you dreamed of. Successful parenting doesn't necessarily follow that pattern. Children, unlike inanimate wood, stone and glass, have personalities of their own and often make choices which can thwart our best intentions for them. So, is it possible that you can do a good job as a parent but your child's behavior disappoint you? Is it possible for a child to do well in spite of the poor parenting of those to whom he is entrusted?

These are interesting questions. My work with people over many decades causes me to answer "yes" to both. While parents are the most powerful people in a young child's life they are not all powerful for their entire life. Some children make wise choices and learn to build their lives upon the love and nurture of their parents.

> *While parents are the most powerful people in a young child's life they are not all powerful for their entire life.*

Others, nurtured by good parents also, become victims of their own poor choices. Some not so fortunate to have functional parents manage to overcome many of the unhealthy habits and thought patterns of their parents to become much healthier in relationships than would seem possible.

Melody's story is testimony that miracles still happen. She is not the same out-of-control, anxiety-ridden young woman who appeared in my office a few years ago. When I first met her she was struggling in her job, worried about making ends meet and frustrated in her relationships with men.

As the weeks and months unfolded she told me of the neglect and emotional abuse she suffered as a child. This brave and resourceful young woman has worked hard to counter the major deficit she inherited from her parents. Hers is a story of grace, faith and miracle.

Melody's parents were highly dysfunctional and, unfortunately for her and her siblings, created obstacles rather than teaching them to live a healthy life. Melody's biological father abandoned the family when she was only three years old and was later imprisoned for a felony.

Her mother remarried and brought another abusive man into their lives. Melody and her siblings lived in constant fear of the stepfather and often witnessed fights and physical abuse between the parents. Being the oldest, Melody became the protector and caretaker of the younger children and assumed the role of the responsible adult in the family. The environment in which she grew up lacked the safety and love she needed for a positive view of herself and left her fearful of trusting anyone else, especially men. Managing to get through high school, she escaped the family and moved to a nearby town to work. This was a turning point for Melody. While attending a church there she met a couple who offered to let her stay with them while she worked. This was her first up close experience with a functional family and the experience with them over the next four years gave her more acceptance and care than she had ever known. While with this family shecompleted her college degree and established a life of her own. After leaving these surrogate parents she earned a master's degree and has maintained a close relationship with them. Melody struggled for some time to find her professional niche but has become quite a successful entrepreneur and owns her own small business.

She is one of the clients I have admired and respected most in all my years of counseling. She has been able through faith and personal determination to develop her own identity while maintaining a respectful relationship with family members who are still stuck in their dysfunctional patterns. Her greatest struggle has been to overcome her fear of the vulnerability involved in a relationship with a man. However, characteristic of the grit and determination which has marked so much of her life she hasn't given up on her dream of a family.

Melody's story has just demonstrated for you what successful parenting is not. In spite of her parents, Melody has become quite healthy and successful. I believe she is more the exception than the rule, the miracle rather than what usually happens. Although she deserved better, it is likely she will deal with some of the vestiges of her early years for the rest of her life. While it is true that tremendous struggles can produce character it is unfortunate and unnecessary that Melody's parents are the ones responsible for her pain. Life has enough difficulties through which we can grow without having to overcome your parents' stuff along the way. All children deserve better but do not get to choose their parents.

This brings me to my definition of successful parenting. Successful parenting is providing an environment in which a child feels loved and is safe to become all God intended him to be. The emphasis in this approach is influence, not control. Your job as a parent is to know your child and to encourage him and make it possible for him to develop to his full potential. You have succeeded as a parent when you provide this environment for growth. What your child does with the opportunity is not your responsibility.

> *Successful parenting is providing an environment in which a child feels loved and is safe to become all God intended him to be.*

The reason I define success this way is because I firmly believe it is not our job to change other people but to create an environment conducive to change. Direct attempts to change a person end in frustration and resentment and any perceived success is only temporary. Real change and growth must come from deep within a person, from inside out. We are to guide our children toward what we believe is best for them but ultimately they must choose the course they will take.

> *Real change and growth must come from deep within a person, from inside out.*

In the following chapters I will attempt to help you understand the major issues of parenting and offer guidelines to developing a warm and caring relationship with your child. It is my belief that your relationship with your child will provide the understanding and tools necessary for him to grow into a confident, caring and responsible person.

This book, PARENTING WITH A PURPOSE, is the product of my deeply rooted conviction that life has a divine purpose and parents are to train their children according to that purpose. As you read further you will see that Scripture clearly supports my premise.

I am now in the seventh decade of my life and have accumulated, I believe, a fair amount of understanding about children and what they need. Some of this understanding has been from reading, much through failures, lots through the emotional suffering I've observed in clients and a great deal through a consistent study of Scripture through much of my lifetime. The teachings of Scripture form the foundation of my understanding of the meaning of life and God's direction for us to be the people He created us to be.

One of the major challenges of parenting is that it is on the job training. We take the examples of our parents, books or articles we have read, perhaps a course in child development and we set out on this marvelous and scary journey of trying to guide the life of another human being. Parenting can be a daunting task and it is my hope as you read this book you will gain clarity of direction and some insight into how to handle the practical issues of everyday life with your child. Most importantly, I hope you will ask the Lord for wisdom on a daily basis, find encouragement to grow through your mistakes and enjoy this wonderful experience of helping your child's life unfold before God.

To enhance the readability and helpfulness of the book I have included materials from case work I have done through the years. All names and some details have been changed to protect the identity and confidentiality of these persons. However, the essential issues of the cases have not been altered in order to demonstrate the particular concern being addressed.

PART ONE

THE BIG PICTURE

CHAPTER ONE

THE PURPOSE

John struggled with many issues in his personal life and marriage. But in this particular session he wanted to talk about his problems with Amanda, his teenage daughter. She had grown increasingly disrespectful in her talk and actions and he wanted to know how to fix her. What I discovered was he had never allowed himself to be vulnerable enough to develop a close relationship with her. Now that she was acting out he was working from a real deficit and his control tactics and position as her father carried little weight with her. I pleaded with him, as I have with few clients, to open his heart to her and fight for a positive relationship. Unfortunately, he wouldn't do the hard work required and the relationship continued to deteriorate.

What I was really challenging John to consider is what is at the heart of parenting. Parenting is about relationships and all that makes them work right. John

Parenting is about relationships and all that makes them work right.

wanted a relationship on his terms and was unwilling to do the really hard work to fix the only person he could fix, himself.

Most of the people who come to my office have at least one thing in common. They are there because they are experiencing the pain of a dysfunctional relationship. Many, like John, have an inadequate or misguided view of themselves which can cause all sorts of problems in relationships. This issue of a distorted self-image is so pervasive that it would be difficult to overestimate the poison and negative impact it has on people's lives.

Many come to see me because their marriage is coming apart. Max, now in his second marriage, painted this word picture. " I see this rope being stretched tightly from both ends. And the rope is starting to fray and some of the strands are breaking. It's only a matter of time until the whole rope snaps." That's a scary thought if you are sitting in Max's chair. Again, this is an issue of relationships and how to make them work.

Still others seek my help because life has thrown them a curve, been unfair and doesn't make sense. Some have been sorely disappointed with God for not fulfilling their dreams or expectations and come seeking a new sense of direction and purpose in life. Life had truly been unfair to Brenda. She had attempted to make the changes her husband wanted and had suffered through his "mid-life crisis" only to discover he was having an affair during the time they were in counseling together. They had started out in marriage together as believers but along the way his financial success and an unresolved personal problem with self-image destroyed the marriage. There was nothing Brenda could do to save it. Thankfully, Brenda was grounded enough in her relationship with God that she has been able to deal with her disappointment and grief without abandoning her faith.

I have given these examples to illustrate the three dimensions of relations, that of self, others and God. How we relate to self, others and God is what life is about. The degree to which we do this in a functional way determines our personal growth and our relative success in what really matters in life. So, parenting is about helping our child grow and mature in his relationship with himself, others and God. Why do I say this?

> *How we relate to self, others and God is what life is about.*

My belief that the main job of parents is building foundations and bridges for relationships comes directly from the Bible. While many references could be cited to support this concept the one most prominent to me is Matthew 22:34-40. Let me tell you a little bit about it. An expert in the law has challenged Jesus to identify the greatest of all the commandments in hopes of trapping him in a theological error. The Lord's replay is amazing in that he summarized the ultimate meaning of all the law as well as the prophets in this succinct statement:

"'Love the Lord your God with all your heart and with all your soul and with all your mind.' This is the first and greatest commandment. And the second is like it: 'Love your neighbor as yourself.' All the law and prophets hang on these two commandments."

God has given us his commandments and all the teachings of Scripture to point us to his purpose in life. That purpose for every human being is to love. God is to be the supreme object of our love. And Jesus so connects this idea with the next that he makes the second part inseparable from the first. To love God one must also love others as he loves himself. The lack of understanding and applying this fact has been a source of disgrace in the lives of many who claim Jesus as Lord. The fact is that our true love for God is shown by how we treat others.

And how we treat others is really a strong clue as to the health of our love for our self.

> *a proper love for oneself is the foundation of emotional health and functional relationships.*

It is highly important that we not miss an underlying assumption in Jesus' statement about loving others. We are to love others as we love our self. In my work as a therapist I have found that a proper love for oneself is the foundation of emotional health and functional relationships. When that component is missing or badly damaged the capacity to love others and God is compromised, at best, or completely absent. George came to me in an effort to save his marriage. His contact was prompted by the fact he had spent the night in jail for hitting his wife. Work with him revealed he was a very angry and negative person. He had been so damaged by his father's abandonment and his mother's promiscuous lifestyle that he believed everyone was against him, including God. He made poor decisions with money and work issues and when things didn't go right he concluded that God didn't love him and was actually working against him. He believed he was worthless and the choices he made often led to his expectation of failure. George was a difficult person to care for but his wife and members of his church group made a real effort which helped. However, the main person who needed to love George was George.

While this example of the absence of self- love in George's life may seem to be extreme I use it to make a critical point. Your child's ability to love God and others as he should is dependent on a proper love for himself. So, the first part of your job as a parent is to provide an environment where your child is loved unconditionally. If he truly experiences love he will learn to love himself. There will be more detail on this in chapter five.

The power and influence of parents on a young life are unmistakable. The child comes into the world totally dependent on the good will of the parents and as he grows he attempts to make whatever adjustments he perceives necessary to have their attention and approval. His belief about himself is a reflection of how he interprets his experiences of life with his parents. Parents are the "mirror" into which he looks to get a sense of his worth.

As a parent you have the primary position and responsibility in helping your child find life's true meaning; love of self, God and others. You can choose to do your best to provide an environment to help this happen. It is hard work but there is no better investment you can make.

> *You are the first human bridge to your child's acceptance of the fact that God loves him.*

Before closing this discussion on your most important job let's do a brief overview of relationships in your child's future. As a believer you would probably say that you want your child to know God and accept Jesus as his savior, right? To love God supremely is the most important issue of life. But please understand that we are not talking about a formula your child must follow but a relationship with God. This is not just going to church and learning "about" God. While those things are good they are no substitute for knowing God personally. 1 John 1:16 says "God is love." The very character of God is love and your role as a parent is to demonstrate love to your child even before he can begin to understand that God exists or that God loves him. You are the first human bridge to your child's acceptance of the fact that God loves him. God uses the love of human beings to bring others into a personal relationship with himself. Those people who serve as a bridge to God have developed a capacity to love.

Other relationships in your child's future have to do with you and other members of the family, friends, people of authority such as teachers, and possibly a life mate. Learning how to love these people will have much to do with your child's success in school, friendships, career and a family of his own. Giving your child a good foundation in how to love others will bless him throughout his life.

The relationship which is at the core of your work as a parent is your child's relationship to himself. How you address this will set the direction for how he will relate to others and ultimately to God. This is primarily what I want to address in this book. And to this we now turn our attention.

CHAPTER TWO

WHERE DO I BEGIN?

I talked with someone recently who began a project and realizing the instructions were missing attempted it anyway. He was not happy. It took much longer than it should have and he made mistakes he had to go back and correct. Has this ever happened to you? If so, you know how frustrating and impossible a task can be without some direction about where to begin and the successive steps to follow.

Parenting can be a very complicated and difficult task. It is a job given to each of us the moment a child comes into our life. There was no instruction book with mine and I'm quite sure you didn't get one either. After the thrill and joy of bringing a new life in the world subsides a little you are faced with how you are going to rear them. So, you consult your pediatrician, mom and others for advice on how to handle the physical issues of caring for a new baby. However, there is much more to being a good parent than physical care and the more daunting issue of being a good "psychological parent" remains to be worked out in the years ahead.

While having a baby makes you a parent it doesn't make you a good one. A person is not somehow magically transformed into a mature, caring person because they have a baby. While the physical care of a baby is very important and must be addressed the long term issue of parenting is who you are as a person. This is the place to begin, your character. **Yes, character does matter. And there is no place in life where it matters more than in parenting.**

having a baby makes you a parent it doesn't make you a good one

I think of character as the sum total of traits and habits which make us who we are. Everyone has character and those habits and traits can have a profound effect on a child. What do you think of when you remember some of the people you most admire? Perhaps some of the following words would describe their character: integrity, truthful, caring, dependable, punctual, self-disciplined, resourceful, patient, thoughtful, thrifty, friendly, and encouraging. All these are characteristics which promote good relationships. There are also negative terms to describe people whose actions and attitudes destroy relationship. Words such as dishonest, selfish, uncaring, immature, childish, explosive, impulsive, stingy, stubborn, dependent, anxious and bitter describe a negative and destructive character. Likely you

Yes, character does matter. And there is no place in life where it matters more than in parenting.

are a person, like most of us, with some qualities or traits on both lists. It is helpful to have a pretty realistic view of yourself so you can continue to develop the good qualities and also address the effect of the negative ones on yourself, your child and others. Thankfully, character is something that can be changed with insight, time and effort.

One my clients gradually began to see the destructive toll her anger and immaturity were taking on her daughter. Her words reflect the pain of many who have come to such a place of awareness.

"I want my daughter to grow up feeling better about herself than I did growing up. But how can I help her with that if I don't feel good about myself?"

The truth is you cannot teach your child something you don't have deep inside yourself. Unkind parents cannot raise kind children. Undisciplined parents cannot raise disciplined children. Self-centered parents cannot raise children who care about others. Who you are is what you really teach your children because your actions express your core values. You cannot separate who you are from the way you approach parenting.

The following two Scriptures identify the fact that our manner of life proceeds from attitudes deep within us. In the "heart" reside the values, aspirations and commitments to which we give our time and effort.

"Above all else, guard your heart, for it is the wellspring of life" Proverbs 4:23

"The good man brings good things out of the good stored up in his heart, and the evil man brings evil things out of the evil stored up in his heart. For out of the overflow of his heart his mouth speaks." Luke 6:45

Who you are at the heart or core of your being is how you will live your life and how you will raise your child. Although you may differ from your parents in many ways it may amaze you to notice the similarity of attitudes and values that have remained through the years. Any changes you have sought to make have not come easily. Just as the environment of your home shaped you in many ways your home has the potential of shaping your child.

For a number of years the following words had a prominent place on our refrigerator to remind me and my wife of the power of our character in the lives of our children.

If a child lives with criticism, he learns to condemn.
If a child lives with hostility, he learns to fight.
If a child lives with ridicule, he learns to be shy.
If a child lives with shame, he learns to feel guilty.
If a child lives with tolerance, he learns to be patient.
If a child lives with encouragement, he learns confidence.
If a child lives with praise, he learns to appreciate.
If a child lives with fairness, he learns justice.
If a child lives with security, he learns to have faith.
If a child lives with approval, he learns to like himself.
If a child lives with acceptance and friendship, he learns to find love in the world. (Author unknown)

The following questions are designed to help you evaluate yourself regarding some of the areas which are highly significant in building healthy relationships with your child.

1. Do you love people based on the way they treat you? Always   most of the time   sometimes   never .

2. Do you struggle with delaying gratification for a long term benefit? Never   sometimes   often   always.

3. Do you depend on others to make you feel good about yourself? Never   sometimes   often   always.

4. Do you function on your own in a healthy way while still maintaining good interdependent relationships with others? Always   sometimes   rarely   never.

5. How do you rate your communication skills in talking and listening to others? Excellent good   fair   poor.

You will discover the importance of these questions in the chapters which follow. To help you remember them I would like to issue a challenge to you. Ask someone who will be absolutely truthful with you to rate you on these questions and explain why they answered as they did.

Let me, even at the risk of being redundant, stress the importance of your character in your child's life. Hopefully, one of the following images will cause you to see your role in a way you have never seen it before. You are your child's most influential TEACHER. You are God's primary way of teaching him what really matters in life. Who you are, what you say and do are important. You are a BRIDGE BUILDER. You are a vital link to your child's relationship to himself, God and others. You are a MAP MAKER. Your life and character provides your child with direction to life that lies in front of him. The choices you make determine your character and influences your child in many ways.

There is a sense in which we are now dealing with the toughest issue in parenting, that of our own personal demons which need to be recognized and extracted. All the knowledge and latest techniques to change your child's behavior are of little value if you fail to deal with the "baggage" which keeps you from being the emotional/spiritual parent your child needs you to be.

Charles and Marge came to see me because they were having marital problems and also could not agree on how to deal with their eight- year- old daughter's behavior. Charles found it impossible to please Marge. Even though he pampered her and tried to give her everything she wanted she was not happy. She saw him as the problem and any attempt to explore her contribution to their issues met with resistance. Making no headway on her agenda frustrated her and she quit therapy after a few sessions. He continued for a while but quit later, realizing it takes two people to fix a marriage. Thankfully, the story doesn't end here. Several months passed before I would see them again. At the close of a seminar where I spoke in their church and I saw Marge making her way toward me. I didn't know what to expect from her since she had left counseling so dissatisfied with my work with them. But as she approached me she smiled and we made a few courteous remarks and then I asked her, " Well, Marge, how's your family?" She replied, "We're just doing great, the best we've ever been." A bit surprised by her answer I said, "That's great. Why is that?" "Because," she said, "I decided to grow up." What a beautiful answer to the most difficult of all parenting issues. It is about growing up.

> *God meets us at the point of our effort*

Maybe your attempt to understand yourself and deal with any challenges you may encounter will cause you to begin journaling as a means of clarifying the issues and their beginnings. Perhaps you will seek the counsel of a good book or attend a seminar on a particular subject with which you struggle. Or you may seek the help of a pastoral counselor or other therapist to help you sort out and address your concerns. All the above can be helpful. The important thing is that you make effort to make the needed changes. And remember, God meets us at the point of our effort. It is as James 1:5 says "If any of you lacks wisdom, he should ask God, who gives generously without finding fault, and it will be given to him."

CHAPTER THREE

Own Your Stuff

I wanted to be a perfect parent just like I wanted to believe my parents were perfect. But my children came along and my personal hopes for perfection were challenged and defeated. I quickly learned of my selfishness and immaturity. But it was not until my children were practically grown that I realized my parents didn't have halos either. My fantasies were exposed for what they were and somehow I was okay with that. My parents weren't perfect but they were good enough and I will forever be indebted to them for the love and care they gave me.

Looking back it is rather easy to see ways in which I failed my children. I was often too intense and expected too much. One particularly painful reminder of my imperfection was my seven year old son's response to pressure he was feeling from me. In an attempt to deal with my own anxiety I was pushing him pretty hard on some issue when he stopped me in my tracks. With tears welling up in his eyes, he said to me with a trembling voice,

"Dad, you need to remember I'm only a seven year old kid."

In other words, he was telling me to "lighten up," that I was expecting too much, being too hard on him.

This was a tough moment for me. What do I do with this arrow that has pierced my heart? Do I shoot it back at him? Do I take it and remain silent and let him wonder if he is going to have to pay for this honest expression of feelings? I was so startled by his honesty that I actually allowed myself to listen to him. My tone changed from demanding to penitent and my reply was, "Nathan, you're right. I am being too hard on you and I'm sorry."

That was a great lesson for me and in many ways helped me to be more aware and careful about projecting my anxieties onto my children. It was also a helpful experience for Nathan. You'll learn why a little bit later.

In my counseling work I've met countless neurotic parents like myself. They are overly careful, feeling somehow they will ruin their child if they make mistakes. Don't worry, you won't ruin them and recovering from the mistake can help you be more understanding of yourself and cement a really solid relationship with your child. But not dealing with the illusion of perfection can have devastating results on a child.

Maggie was an attractive but troubled teenager who was brought to me by a notable professional man and his wife. I knew of the man by reputation only and was quite flattered that he would seek my help. I thought of him as highly successful with all the accompanying amenities, a big beautiful house, new cars and plenty of money from his business. Maggie was causing real problems getting drunk and embarrassing the family. The family image was being threatened and Maggie was the reason and so I was given the job to fix her.

As Maggie began to open up to me I became increasingly aware that her behavior was really a symptom of an underlying problem in the family. She was the scapegoat, the identified patient, but the real issue was her parents. Some of the most revealing sessions were when she would talk about her loneliness and how neither parent really tried to listen to her. Maggie was quite insightful and was hurt by the idea that her parents were more interested in appearance than in what was really going on. Maggie was acting out as a cry for help and understanding.

In my rare visits with them, neither parent would not, could not entertain the idea that something they were doing or not doing was part of the issue. They had an agenda to "fix" her and that would solve the problem.

In a session just before I was fired by the parents Maggie explained the family in a word picture which I have never forgotten. She described it like this,

"At a distance you see this beautiful car. Everything is pretty and shiny but as you get closer you realize everything is not what it seems to be. Looking inside the car you see that it is a mess, all junked up and not at all what it appears to be."

Maggie's parents weren't bad people. They just had their priorities in the wrong place. Their anxiety about appearing successful and all that went with that image had diverted their attention from their daughter. By doing so they had failed Maggie and let her carry their personal issues. My strong hunch is that Maggie was dealing with the dysfunctional issues in their marriage which they had failed to admit and address. I believe we were getting too close to the real issues when they terminated the counseling.

One of the most important things I've learned in rearing my own children and counseling many others is that owning your own stuff really helps your child. Let me tell you why I think this. As a parent you hold an important and powerful place in your child's life. In your child's early years with you she believes you

owning your own stuff really helps your child.

are all-powerful and can do no wrong. You are always right, perfect. Of course, the only problem with this idea is that it is wrong. You're not perfect. You do have wrong ideas. You do make mistakes. So, when you deny your issues the way Maggie's parents did your child has to do something with the conflict this creates inside her. Sometimes, as in Maggie's case, the child becomes discouraged, develops a low self- esteem and chooses behavior that is destructive. Maggie made bad choices which could harm her and embarrassed her family. However, she made those choices in rebellion against parents whom she believed loved their image of success more than they loved her. Had they been successful in the things that really matter?

Another person who comes to mind is Julia. She is forty, petite and a people pleaser. She likes everyone to be happy even if it means swallowing her own feelings. She has a difficult time acknowledging her feelings, especially the negative ones, and dealing with them. After several sessions with me she was able to see where the problem began. The source of the issue dates back to her early years when she felt she needed to "walk on eggshells" to keep from setting off her dad's anger. This fear drove her to find a way to stay emotionally safe. Like most children in this situation she didn't understand what was really happening and chose a response which would keep the "peace" but didn't work in the long run. Her way to avoid conflict was to repress her anger and frustration with her dad. Consequently, she began pushing down lots of her feelings especially if she felt they would make someone uncomfortable or lead to conflict. This pattern started when she was a child and has continued well into her adult life. Julia's plan didn't change him and it hasn't worked for her either.

Being a "pleaser" has had an up side for Julia in her job. Everybody likes the fact that she will go the extra mile to do whatever needs to be done. But her avoidance of conflict also has a major downside. Julia gets tired of carrying this heavy load of expectations after a while and becomes exhausted and depressed. Her fear keeps her from addressing some of the issues with her boss and coworkers and once she is able to regain some balance she goes back to doing what she has done all her life. She denies her feelings and pretends everything is wonderful but deep inside she is really miserable. Her depression worsens with each recurring episode.

What might have happened in her growing up years if her dad had owned his anger and apologized for the suffering and misery he had caused her? She would have been set free from the prison she was building to keep her safe. But he never apologized and her mother just ignored his behavior. Now, at forty, Julia is beginning to realize her strategy for keeping her safe has created a trap which is much worse than the one she was trying to avoid.

> *The correct use of authority builds healthy and respectful relationships with children.*

As parents we need to own our stuff and make amends with our child wherever possible. Some parents seem to think and act as if an apology somehow weakens their authority with their child. The self-talk probably goes something like this, "If I admit I was wrong she won't respect me and I'll lose all control of her." This kind of wrong thinking often produces wrong actions. Apologizing doesn't weaken your authority with your child. Neither does having authority mean you are always right. Paul gives a very strong warning in Ephesians 6:4 about the misuse of our authority. The correct use of authority builds healthy and respectful relationships with children. The prideful, wrong use of authority can destroy them.

One way to think about whether or not an apology is needed is to ask, "If I had treated my boss or a friend the way I treated my child should I apologize to them?" If the answer is yes then your child deserves one also. We should treat our child's feelings like they are important to us and act accordingly. When we have been wronged by someone an apology goes a long way in restoring our trust in that person. The same is true for our child.

One of the issues I have faced in this area has been that I have often been both right and wrong in situations with my children. For example, I was right to be concerned, frustrated or angry about a situation but wrong in the way I handled it. I allowed my anger or impatience to take charge and instead of correcting the problem I made it worse by saying or doing something inappropriate. In situations such as this an apology was not necessary for my concern over the issue but for how I handled it.

So, what do you do when you make blunders with your child? Here are some ideas you may want to consider.

First, acknowledge your mistake. Own it and don't make excuses for you actions.

Second, consider an apology. If the mistake took place in a direct way with your child or has a direct effect on him an apology is needed. A broken promise or misuse of anger would be examples of this. I believe Julia's and Maggie's parents owed them apologies for their actions because they created dysfunctional situations their children were unable to handle.

Third, learn from your mistakes. True apologies are difficult and we should attempt to never have to apologize for the same offence over and over again. This personal embarrassment added to the greater need to protect our child from our negative behavior should push us to fix our problem.

And finally, forgive yourself and move on. Ask God for wisdom to deal with your stuff, deal with it, and give yourself some of the grace God and your child give you.

CHAPTER FOUR

THE GIFT

Where do children come from? This question may seem at first a bit ridiculous but a close examination of various attitudes which underlie some answers to the question will demonstrate its relevance. Why is your attitude about where children come from so important? Because your attitude determines the approach you will take toward your child and your role in relation to him. It is highly likely your child will sense your attitude in a thousand little ways and will value himself according to what he interprets your feeling toward him to be. A child tends to feel about himself the way he perceives his parents feel about him. While you can't completely control your child's attitude toward himself you can do much to set him on the path to a positive view of himself.

> *A child tends to feel about himself the way he perceives his parents feel about him.*

Now, let's examine a few options to answering the question, "Where do children come from?"

Children are the result of a sexual relationship between a man and a woman. Of course, this is undeniably true. But is this the complete answer? Those who see this as the answer may cherish the "miracle" they have created and care deeply for the child but they recognize no First Cause or Creator. To them God has no connection to them and their child. While they may accept responsibility to be good parents, a vital aspect of parenting is missing: the privilege of consciously working with God to direct this new life.

To assume that a child is nothing more than the result of a sexual relationship can lead to a much more tragic conclusion than that just described. Some people believe that since they made the baby they can dispose of it. This attitude, unfortunately, leads to thousands of children's lives being ended by abortion each year.

> *The biblical view is that a child is a gift from God*

A second option is to consider the child an accident. No child needs to be exposed to the cruel statement that they were an "accident." While there is truth to the fact that some children weren't "planned" parents need to take the responsibility for their actions and not burden the child with the feeling he is not wanted. He didn't ask to be born and he deserves to be lovingly accepted and cared for. Does God view the child as an accident? Of course not.

The biblical view is that a child is a gift from God. While accepting responsibility for their sexual relations, couples should also understand that their ability to conceive and have children is a gift from God. It is encouraging to me to see childless couples go through all kinds of expensive medical procedures to have a child. For some these procedures fail and they want a child so badly they adopt. Many times this agonizing process to bring a child into their life takes years. They see a child as a gift and blessing in their life. On the other hand, I am a bit puzzled to see some couples who seem to be very prolific in producing children have a "so what" attitude about it.

I am convinced that one of the most important ingredients in being a Christian parent is the unmistakable certainty a child is a gift from God. This attitude is well supported in Scripture and blessed indeed is the child whose parents believe it and act it out in their relationship with him.

> *one of the most important ingredients in being a Christian parent is the unmistakable certainty a child is a gift from God*

Consider the following biblical concepts as you think about where your child came from.

The ability to procreate is a blessing from God. Genesis 1:28 says concerning Adam and Eve, "God blessed them and said to them, 'Be fruitful and increase in number; fill the earth and subdue it.'" The biblical view is that the ability to reproduce children is a blessing from God. It is not a cosmic accident but the plan of God for human happiness and his purposes. Think about that in a personal sense. Your child is God's gift to you.

Psalm 127:3 is just one of many references to the fact that a child is a gift from God. Think about your child as you read this. "Sons are a heritage from the Lord, children a reward from him..."

Few, if any cultures, have valued children as much as the Hebrews. The Psalmist gives the strong impression that a man's wealth and strength were measured by the number of children he had. Psalm 127:4-5 reads as follows, "Like arrows in the hands of a warrior are sons born in one's youth.

Blessed is the man whose quiver is full of them." On the other hand, couples who could not have children considered themselves as somehow lacking life's greatest blessing. Out of this rich background we, as Christians, should approach the experience of parenting with a special sense of wonder, awe and gratitude for the gift of a child.

"Are we rich?" How would you answer that question if your child were to ask you? I well remember the morning when Nathan, about ten, posed it to me. Kristen, his younger sister, overheard the question and her curiosity brought her close so she could hear the verdict. We had recently purchased a car and I knew this had probably begun the wheels turning in their minds. Kids like the idea of being rich for some reason. Well, my approach went something like this. "We have everything we need. While we don't have lots of money we're rich. Know why? Because your mom and I have the two of you and that makes us rich." That was one of the best answers I was ever to give to all the questions they fired at me through the years!

Some months later I was reassured that sometimes your children really take to heart what you tell them. Kristen and I were talking about possessions when she remarked, "Daddy, we're rich aren't we? You know why? 'Cause you've got me and Nathan." My deepest aspirations as a dad were touched that moment as my beautiful little girl put into words the thought of her great worth to the most important people in her life.

One of the most important insights you will ever have about your child is that he is a gift from God. This belief, this attitude is basic to all you must attempt to do for them. God made your child and gave him and placed him in your care for a little while.

Have you ever thought about why God gives parents children? Obviously children keep the human race going but is there more to the gift than that? As a parent and grandparent I believe God has given me children and grandchildren to enhance my life. They are a personal gift to make my life better and more meaningful. Think about what God may be trying to do for you by giving you the gift of a child. Here are three things I will suggest God does for us by giving us children. .

First, God gives us children to enhance our relationship to himself. While parents are teachers, we are to be learners also. In many ways God uses our children to remind us that he cares for us. In some of those special moments when we seem almost overwhelmed by our love for our child we also realize that God loves us beyond our ability to comprehend. It is not by coincidence that Jesus uses loving family terms to describe the believer's relationship to God. He tells us to speak to God in intimate language: "Our Father in heaven…" (Matthew 6:9).

It is through our child that we see complete trust and dependence demonstrated. They show us how our heavenly Father wants us to trust him! Our young child doesn't worry about the necessities of life. He trusts his parents to provide what he needs. The idea of the child teaching the parent the meaning of trust must have been in the mind of Jesus in the following illustration:

'Which of you, if his son asks him for bread, will give him a stone? Or if he asks for a fish, will give him a snake? If you, then, though you are evil, know how to give good gifts to your children, how much more will your Father in heaven give good gifts to those who ask him! (Matthew 7:9-11).

If we are flawed and make mistakes and our children can trust us how much more can we trust our heavenly Father to do what is best for us. God uses our children to remind us of this great truth.

Second, God uses our children to renew our wonder about life. The stress and strain of life can zap the joy and wonder out of us and we can forget that life itself is a miracle.

Holding a newborn or looking into the wonderstruck eyes of a child exploring the world around him can uncover that joy about life that has been buried under the worries and pressures of daily living. Taking time to see the world through the eyes of your child can help you sense the awesome power and greatness of our loving Creator and Lord.

Third, God uses our children to renew our hope about life. Even as you read these words there is trouble throughout the world. Natural disasters, military action and human suffering are common in many areas of our world. The threat of nuclear war hangs over our world and the future doesn't seem very promising. Why would thinking people bring children into a world like this?

For the believer, having children can be a statement of hope and faith. Rearing children to serve the Lord offers a ray of hope for the world. If God had considered only the social, political and economic conditions in first century Israel He would have never have allowed Jesus to be born when He was.

There is a real sense in which having children is an act of worship and ministry for the Christian. Those who seek God's guidance and blessing in having and rearing children can bring to the world a person who can make a great contribution for good.

> *There is a real sense in which having children is an act of worship and ministry for the Christian.*

There is one final question I want you to consider before we bring this subject of the child as a gift to a close. What do you do with this gift from God? Think about the child or children God has given you and see if the following suggestions seem appropriate to you.

Give thanks for the gift. A gift is something bestowed or given by someone else. It is not earned but is the result of the generosity of someone else directed toward us. It is an expression of the giver's care for the person receiving it. We cannot and should not try to repay the giver for the gift. The only appropriate response to the giver of a gift is gratitude.

When God gives a couple the unparalleled gift of a child the response should be one of gratitude and worship. Other than one's personal relationship to God and one's mate, nothing can rival the value of a child. Celebration, thanksgiving and joy are in order!

Remember the Giver. Just to the right of my computer screen on my desk is an engraved clock given by friends a number of years ago. It not only serves to remind me of the time but of a meaningful relationship. Warm memories of good times together come easily as I think about the givers. In every room of my house there are tangible reminders of my contact with people over the years. A picture over the table, a flower arrangement, a radio, a candleholder, an oil lamp; all these and many more evoke memories of different times and caring relationships.

> *When God gives a couple the unparalleled gift of a child the response should be one of gratitude and worship.*

My children, Nathan and Kristen, were and remain this day reminders of the relationship my wife and I have with each other and with God. The names we gave them and the way we tried to rear them signified our consciousness that they were gifts from our loving heavenly Father. We realized we were blessed to have them and attempted to honor God as a way of thanking Him for them.

One way you can demonstrate your thankfulness to God for your child is to privately and publicly acknowledge it. You can demonstrate your gratitude to God through prayer and conversation in your home. Begin at an early age to include your child in these activities and allow them to see you express your love for God and for them. You can publicly remember

God as the giver of your child through a dedication service for you and your child. In this way you make a statement to others that you believe God has placed this child in your care.

Be a good parent. You have been entrusted with a very valuable gift and the way you treat it says a lot about you. Accepting responsibility for the spiritual, physical, emotional, social, and intellectual needs of your child is where good parenting begins. Some gifts need no further attention than placing them in a prominent place and an occasional dusting. However, this is not true with children. They are not finished products by any means and this is where your major work is. They need you to lovingly guide them toward the true meaning of life. You no longer belong to just yourself and your mate. You have a gift from God to care for. You belong to your child and your child belongs to you.

Enjoy your gift. While children come with lots of work and responsibility they are also a great joy. Please don't lose the sense of enjoyment in being their parent. Children bring excitement to life and the things they say and do will be your gifts to treasure through the years. Take pleasure in them, enjoy them, play with them, grow with them. If you will allow them to do so, your children will help you rediscover the true joy of being alive. Parenting has a great number of wonderful joys for you to discover. I hope you find every one of them.

CHAPTER FIVE

HEALTHY LOVE

Are there good and bad ways to" love" a child? See what you think after reading the following story.

Mike's mother was deeply attached to him. His older brother had died soon after birth and when Mike was born his mom showered him with all her attention. As he grew and expressed independence, she still insisted on doing everything for him. She reluctantly let him go to school and often reminded him of how much she missed him and wished he was home. Mike didn't adjust to school well and refused to participate in activities which challenged his shyness. Inside him there was a growing dislike for school and when he finished the ninth grade he decided he had had enough and quit. His mom and dad didn't insist he finish school. Although it would appear selfish to say it openly his mom was glad to have her little boy home with her. Well into his adult years Mike has been limited by a lack of confidence and by his dependence on others to do for him what he should be doing for himself. No one would ever think to question this mother's devotion to her son. She loved him deeply and that was obvious to all who knew her. If she loved him so much why did he develop traits which in some ways have rendered him quite dysfunctional and dependent on others? Is it possible she meant to love him well but did him harm by her type of love? Was what she did really love or a rather harmful form of emotional attachment? I see Mike's story over and over again in those whose parents were confused as to the real meaning of parent love. We can sincerely care for our child, feel close to them but hurt them in the name of love. There are bad ways to "love" our child and the emotional toll on them can be severe and long-term.

Let's consider several ideas about what a healthy love for our child is not. This will move us in the direction of defining what parent love is and does for a child.

Love is not a feeling or emotion. There is no question that feelings can be an accompaniment to love but love is much more than a feeling. Why do I say this? Because lots of people are confused about the whole issue of feelings and allow their feelings to control them and their actions with their child. When this happens the child is" loved" by the parent when he has done something to elicit good feelings but "not loved" when meeting his needs are inconvenient or his actions are frustrating to the parent. A child reared by such an emotionally immature parent feels he must earn the feeling of being loved by "walking on eggshells' and always being sure not to be any trouble. He cannot risk being himself and being real because his parent cannot deal with it.

Love is not about being best friends. Some children are easier to like than others. They are winsome and happy and easy to be around. When they are hurting or have caused trouble it can be a temptation to be their best friend instead of their parent. This can happen when you are in a difficult place in your marriage, have problems at your job, or just feel lonely. One of things that can happen is that the parent will not only listen to the child but will actually tell the child about their own hurts and use the child to take care of themselves emotionally. This can trap your child into a position with which he should never be burdened, that of taking care of you, the parent.

While we should maintain a friendly relationship with our child we need to keep the lines clear as to who is the parent and who is the child. Our job is to be the adult and to assist our child to grow to be as healthy and functional as possible. You can certainly be your child's friend so long as you understand that role is part of being the parent. Sometimes this will mean your child won't like your decisions and certainly not claim you as their friend. You must be emotionally mature enough to deal with their displeasure without giving in to their demands. In the growing up stages what your child needs most is a parent. Being best friends as parent and child needs to be reserved for the time both of you are mature enough to handle it.

Love is not giving my child what he wants. I see parents play this game often where there is a divorce. It goes something like this. The dad had an affair and the marriage ends in a divorce. The mom has primary custody with dad having visitation rights every other weekend. She carries most of the load in parenting while he gets an apartment and tends to go on with his life. When the children visit him they go out to eat and he buys them lots of things they ask for. Mom generally cannot carry on this kind of lifestyle because of lack of funds and time constraints. He comes across looking like the good guy in the deal while mom keeps on doing the daily routines of rearing his kids. He is basically giving them what they want out of a sense of guilt over the pain he has caused. Children buy into this easily and help him feel less guilty because they are immature and often want things they don't need. Hopefully, children eventually learn the difference between love and things. As they mature they know love doesn't mean they always get what they want.

Confusing love with getting what you want can also happen in families where the marriage is intact. One parent gives into a child's selfish wishes because they haven't dealt with a sense of deprivation from their own childhood. They want their child to have the bike they never got or to be able to do things they never got to do without regard to the fact that they may be dealing with their own hurt rather than their child's need. Sometimes this same parent may give into a child's tantrums and give him what he demands in order to calm him down. By this lack of parental maturity the unfortunate child learns to get what he wants by bullying his way to his desired goal. In the end the parent sometimes excuses his failure to love well by characterizing his child's actions with a sense of disbelief, "How could he be so selfish and uncaring when I gave him everything he wanted?"

Love is not fulfilling your dreams through your child. While your child is a gift he is not yours to possess, to live through. He is not the means by which you can fulfill your aspirations and make up for the disappointments in your life. He has his own life and purpose and it is not to achieve for you what you could not achieve. Parents need to be aware of this because children will often feel trapped in a career path or some other endeavor in an attempt to please their parents. This was a part of the motivation of my educational efforts but fortunately I came realize the problem in time to really take personal ownership of my education.

I can't remember a time when I didn't consider going to college. This may seem somewhat strange since there were no college graduates on either side of my family. As a matter of fact most of my aunts, uncles and grandparents had not completed high school. Dad could read well, write and do basic math but had only gone through four years of elementary school. Mom loved school but was discouraged in her efforts by her father and only finished the eighth grade, a fact she would lament all her life. My parents struggled financially most of my young life and instilled in me the idea that education was the financial savior and way out of what they had endured. My dad had openly declared his kids would go to college if he had to sell everything he had to do it. Emotionally, I felt there was no choice but to go to college because I wanted so much to please my parents. While their encouragement was great in some ways it had mixed motivations. Sure they wanted me to do well and have a better chance than they did but what I wanted wasn't in the mix. Fortunately, I did like school and the sense of accomplishment and success I felt in the process but there was an underlying anxiety which sometimes overwhelmed me when the work got very demanding. I remember getting so frustrated that I would finally break down and cry and this would seem to settle me down and I could finish my work. This was a pattern for me until one day in my sophomore year of college it dawned on me what was happening. The words came out of my mouth as if I were a child who had just looked at his gifts under the Christmas tree, " I'm going to school for my dad." From that moment I was able to make a clear commitment that my education was about me and for me and the underlying anxiety began to subside.

I have been more fortunate than many who have struggled all their lives to do what their parents wanted and to be what their parents wanted them to be. Many grow old striving to fix their parent's deficit but never receive the sense of approval they so desperately seek. A child needs to belong to himself, to be allowed to learn who he is and his God-given abilities and chart his own course once he is old enough to do so. He needs to pursue his own dreams and not feel obligated to fix the hurts and disappointments of his parents through his life. To attempt to live life for a parent is an emotional dead end street.

The issues I've just noted about what love is not are often created by caring parents whose intentions are admirable but whose actions are misguided by their lack of understanding of themselves and their child. All these actions can set up patterns of behavior and anxieties which can emotionally disable a child and make it difficult for him to be successful in relationships and other pursuits in life. One thing all misguided attempts to love a child have in common is that there is some form of payoff for the parent. At its core this is selfish and harmful to the child.

> *love requires a high degree of personal discipline and maturity.*

By now you have probably concluded that loving your child is not such an easy thing to do. It is not that he doesn't need or deserve your love but truly giving love requires a high degree of personal discipline and maturity. Unfortunately, some adults are incapable of genuinely loving another person because they are stuck in their own childhood needs. This is why I believe the first issue of parenting after understanding the purpose of life is to grow up. Parents who act like children cannot rear children in a healthy environment.

So, how do we know if our love for our child is a healthy love? Love seeks to do what is in the ultimate best interest of another person. I believe you will find this idea compatible with the New Testament concept of love

> *Love seeks to do what is in the ultimate best interest of another person*

described in 1Corinthians 13 and in Jesus' teachings about God's love for us. There are several important implications in this definition for parents.

First, there must be an understanding or judgment about what will best serve your child. Over the course of time what values, skills and attitudes will best equip him for life? This judgment on your part may be contrary to that of much of contemporary society, your parents or other influences. This judgment is unavoidable. Some parents consciously choose to attempt to prepare their child for life while others choose to ignore the issue. That too is a judgment, one which will leave their children in the same fog which surrounds their parents.

To be able to choose what we believe to be in the best interest of our child also implies a certain level of knowledge about the meaning of life itself. It means we choose a certain course of action because we have convictions about life's questions. Is life valuable? What is life's purpose? Are we accountable for the way we live our life? Are there certain character traits that are healthy and to be sought after? What are God's expectations of me as a parent? Obviously, many more questions such as this could be raised. For me, a solid grounding in biblical principles is indispensable for the Christian parent who wishes to do what is best for his child. This not only allows you to know what the Bible teaches about certain issues but allows you to read parenting materials and glean what is helpful while discarding what is in conflict with biblical principles. Biblical principles are the base and to that can be added methods and concepts which will aid you in loving your child.

> *For me, a solid grounding in biblical principles is indispensable for the Christian parent who wishes to do what is best for his child.*

Knowledge of your child is vitally important in knowing how to love him. While your child has similarities to his siblings or other children, in general, there is a true sense in which he is unique. Children reared in the same home experience it differently. This is true for various reasons such as personality differences, individual perception of events in the home, birth order, and the growth of the parent in the parenting process. Therefore, you need to be a student of each child and not assume he or she will be like a brother or sister.

For this reason, what works in disciplining one child may prove ineffective with another.

The bottom line of this is that love is meeting the needs of the individual child. Consider how you can meet your child's needs in the following areas. This is by no means an exhaustive study but only directional in order to help you see the major concerns in each area of your child's growth and development.

PHYSICAL. Your child comes to you from God as a spirit in a body. He comes as the most helpless of all creatures. He can literally do nothing for himself except cry to communicate his discomfort. He is dependent on you to feed him, keep him warm or cool, change his diapers, bathe him, protect him from harm and comfort him when he is frightened or angry. Consistent, loving care for these early physical needs not only help him survive physically but also forms the emotional foundations necessary for him to feel attachment and develop a healthy view of himself.

Some mothers are excellent at dealing with the demands of this first phase of life of the dependent baby but are troubled by the child as he begins to express his independence and doesn't need their constant attention. Once he becomes mobile and can get around on his own the child begins to assert his own will and this is where the fun begins. This growing independence is how God intended it and to try to keep your child physically dependent is to hamper him physically and emotionally. A good rule of thumb here is to allow your child to attend to his own needs, as much as possible, once he able to do so. While he still needs you to prepare his food, he may not need you to feed him. Often your child will give you the clue about wanting to do something for himself or by saying something like, "Me do it." Your task here is to provide only the help your child needs and allow him to do what he can on his own. This applies whether you are teaching him to brush his teeth or parallel park.

What about physical touch? Most young children like to be held and cuddled. Touching them appropriately can convey encouragement and care for them. As they grow older they may become less fond of this. Take the cue from your child in this matter. Little boys often enjoy wrestling and physical exertion with an adult so long as the adult protects them from hurt. Such displays of physical touch are types of affection which can bond children with you. While the types of activities may change through the years doing things such as swimming, bike riding, running and basketball can be mutually enjoyable experiences with your child.

Loving for your child physically is done in three ways: provision, care and skill development. Your child is dependent on you to provide for his basic needs of food, clothing and shelter in order to survive physically. Another aspect of your love for him is your care for his body and its needs for touch, bathing, changing, comforting and feeding. Helping your child learn to care for his body by developing good habits related to nutrition and exercise and develop ordinary physical skills will pay large rewards now and in his future.

INTELLECTUAL. While we normally want to assign this area of our child's development over to the school or church it is clear in Scripture that we have an important role here. Please notice what Deuteronomy 6:6-7 has to say about this.

"These commandments I give you today are to be on your hearts. Impress them on your children. Talk about them when you sit at home and when you walk along the road, when you lie down and when you get up."

Whether your child is home schooled, goes to public or private school is an individual choice and depends on many factors. Whatever the case, you should show support and encourage your child's education and not neglect your role in his intellectual development. Please remember Jesus' statement that we are to love God with all our "mind." The mind certainly involves the intellect.

Doing what is in the best interest of your child involves promoting his intellectual development. Here are some ideas you may want to consider as goals in the helping your child grow toward his intellectual potential.

First, use your home environment and relationship to your child to create a love for learning. Read to them, encourage their curiosity, and provide learning opportunities suitable for their developmental level. Your personal example and joy in learning are indispensable if you expect your child to enjoy learning.

Second, intellectual growth involves the accumulation and application of knowledge which is useful in relationships and conducting the functions necessary to everyday living. As a parent you should provide opportunities for growth in this area and stay involved in your child's educational process to insure he is well educated and can apply his knowledge to life situations.

Third, it is very important for your child's intellectual development to learn how to think and use his mind to solve problems. Your child needs to learn to use his basic knowledge to formulate and decide between options. Giving your child choices and discussing the potential results of those choices is one of the best skills you can help your child develop. Teaching him to think for himself will save him lots of trouble and will save you lots of heartache.

The fourth area of intellectual development is for your child to be able to find information when he needs it. It is not necessary to know the answers to all the questions you will encounter in life. However, it is highly important to be able to find the answers when you don't know the answers. For example, an important skill you can help your child with is the use of the Bible and how to find the answers to important life questions.

SOCIAL. To live in a healthy relationship with others your child will need to develop attitudes towards others and skills which will bring good results. Ahead of you and your child may lie some rough waters to negotiate and your child needs to be prepared. Many parents have a valid concern over the kinds of friends their child will choose. They struggle with the fear their child will be easily misled by another child and get involved in unacceptable activities. This is where a child's good judgment needs to override his desire to be liked or to be a part of the group. The child who has a low self-esteem or is lacking in social skills may be especially vulnerable at this point. Children want to liked and accepted by others and that desire can sometimes be more powerful than the desire to do what you have tried to teach them. Remember, mistakes are just that, a "miss-take" on how a situation should be handled and an opportunity for learning. Please handle mistakes lovingly so your child can learn what to do when faced with similar situations in the future.

Here are some ways in which you can love your child by helping him with good social attitudes and skills. Think of how you may use these with your child.

Treating others with respect is important and begins with respecting yourself. Loving others begins with loving yourself. As you teach your child boundaries by the way you treat them they will learn to respect the boundaries of other children regarding their body, possessions, and feelings.

Teaching children to share and be considerate of others is a gradual process. We may think a young child's unwillingness to share a toy with a younger sibling or another child is a sign they are going to grow up to be selfish. Sometimes a well-meaning parent forces the issue thinking they are teaching the "selfish" child a good lesson. To the contrary, if the child is forced to give out of necessity and not out of freedom this can set up an unhealthy situation. Underlying this issue is the fact that a child cannot truly give what he does not emotionally possess (neither can we) and needs time to let it be his decision. He needs to be allowed to say "no" to the request without this being a big deal. Respecting the ownership of the child will allow him to grow to be less possessive and more giving out of his own initiative.

Your child needs to be friendly with others. This doesn't mean he has to be friends with everyone but he can have an attitude which exhibits courtesy in speaking, listening, and treatment of others. Unfortunately some children, and adults, come across as unfriendly or arrogant when spoken to by failing to speak or acknowledge the other person.

Your child needs to learn how to choose his friends wisely. Life is about making choices and friendships are no exception. This is not about being better than another child but in learning to choose friends who treat you the way you want to be treated. This, like most good things in life comes by making some mistakes and learning from them. The issue of friends becomes critical as your child approaches the teen years.

EMOTIONAL. One of the most neglected but important aspects of loving your child is to love him as an emotional being. One reason for this neglect is that we do not understand what our emotions are or what their purpose is. Didn't God give us emotions? Are they a curse or a blessing? Some are afraid of feelings and try to hide or suppress them. Those who become healthy with their feelings learn to appreciate them for their benefits and use them wisely.

Most of the people who come to my office have significant issues with their emotions. They have either stuffed them or have allowed them to rule their life. Johnny, a fifth grader, was brought to see me by his mom who had become worn out with his defiance and disrespect. He showed little or no signs of such behavior at school or in places other than home. He did some art work for me which indicated he was very angry with both parents. The mom reported his angry behavior to be common whenever he didn't get what he wanted. She also admitted she had not been consistent in dealing with these behaviors. Johnny has learned a very destructive lesson: getting angry, sulking, becoming defiant and disrespectful works. I counseled this mom to love him enough to help him change this pattern by using her example to show him how to handle his anger. I also suggested she consider stiff penalties when he misused his anger

Here are some things Johnny and other children need to learn about feelings:

To have feelings is normal. Some feelings are pleasant and some are not but all feelings are okay.

God gave us feelings to help us. They are a form of energy within us to help us accomplish a task, reward us for a job well done, or to respond to a perceived threat or danger.

Children need to learn to identify different feelings such as happy, angry, sad, satisfied, excited, and disappointed. This is the first step in being able to use our feelings appropriately. Sometimes it is useful to your child to give his feelings a name by saying something such as " Jenny, I know you're sad because it's raining and we can't go to the zoo today."

Children need to learn to connect what they feel with why they feel the way they do. Feelings come as an interpretation of an event, memory or in anticipation of an upcoming situation. Why are they afraid, happy or sad?

Children need their feelings validated. It's okay for a child to be angry at his parent. The truth is you get angry at him too. When a child's feelings aren't heard or accepted he feels ashamed of that part of himself.

Children need to learn acceptable ways to express their feelings. Johnny, for example, needs to know healthy ways to express his anger. He should be allowed to tell his parents he's angry without fear of penalty so long as he is not disrespectful or "physical" with them. In these instances, parents should listen and reflect back to the child what they have said. By doing this parents give the child a means of dealing with a dangerous feeling in a safe and acceptable way.

SPIRITUAL. It is easy to see from considering these developmental areas of children how they overlap and interrelate. The truth is the child is a whole person and looking at these areas separately is simply a way to consider individual aspects of the whole child. One part of the child's life affects the others. For example, when your child is sick he has more difficulty controlling his emotions. When he feels good about himself he tends to do better in social and intellectual pursuits. This kind of interrelatedness is certainly true when we consider the child's spiritual life. His spiritual life is about relationships; how he relates to himself, others and God.

> *Your primary job in the area of spiritual development is to lay foundations for a genuine faith relationship with God.*

As stated earlier the foundation of his spiritual life is how he learns to love himself. How does he come to love himself except through the way in which his physical, intellectual, social and emotional needs are met?

Your primary job in the area of spiritual development is to lay foundations for a genuine faith relationship with God. Your teaching by word and example are powerful forces for good with your child. However, be warned that I'm not talking about just being religious. Many children have been driven away from faith in God by the religious parent who didn't realize the most spiritual thing they could do for their child was love him. Instead of listening they lectured and condemned the child's mistakes. I once heard a young person commenting on his father's overly strict religious practices in this way, "If I'm a Christian I can't have any fun and if that's the way it is I don't want to be one." Unfortunately, this young person threw God out with his father's religion.

Certainly you will want to teach your child the basics of the faith you believe. There is no question but what this can be very important but it is only one part of your task in his spiritual development. The most important spiritual issue is your relationship to God and how you communicate his love and trustworthiness to your child through consistent, caring actions. By this you meet the two most fundamental spiritual needs of your child. First, he comes to feel and know that he is deeply loved and, second, he learns he can trust your love to seek only good for him. This is the spiritual bridge you are building to God for your child. Isn't this the essence of our relationship with God? We know him as a God of love who has made us, provided for us and saved us through the death and resurrection of Jesus. Because his love is trustworthy we trust (faith) him with our life for now and eternity.

PART TWO

PUTTING THE PIECES TOGETHER

CHAPTER SIX

BELOVED

When our son, Nathan, was young his mom would often ask him this question, " If all the little boys in the world lined up and I got to pick anyone I wanted do you know who I would choose?" At his young age Nathan could not conceptualize all the little boys in the world lined up and his mom picking him out but he did get the main idea that he was really important to his mom. I can still hear his giggling, happy "me" in response to her question. When Kristen came along later the same question was often posed to her with the same results. This was just one of many ways we sought to communicate a highly important message to our children: YOU ARE VERY SPECIAL TO US.

While there are many gifts you can give your child there is no substitute for or rival to his sense of being special to you. This gift is one which your child

> *While there are many gifts you can give your child there is no substitute for or rival to his sense of being special to you.*

47

cannot buy or earn nor should he feel compelled to do so. This sense of special favor comes from the heart of the parent, a gift of grace. This gift of feeling accepted, worthy, important, capable, confident, beloved (this positive sense of self) is the cornerstone of emotional and spiritual health. It is that elusive piece we search for to begin putting the puzzle together. When it is in place the other pieces seem to start to fit better.

This sense of "specialness" we seek to instill in our child is not something we can accomplish directly by doing any certain thing. Feeling beloved is a by-product, a result of, or combination of three aspects of your child's life. In other words, there are three ways in which your child's sense of self are developed. Your child's view of his physical self, his sense of accomplishment or defeat and the views of significant others toward him combine to give him a growing awareness of himself as important and special or not important and not special.

PHYSICAL SELF. How your child learns to think about his body and physical functions is very important to him throughout his life. His view of his body will play a major role in how he cares for his body, his general appearance, how he attends to his health and how he deals with bodily changes and the fact that he is a sexual being. Perhaps it is good for us to be reminded that God has created our physical body as the highest of all his creation (Genesis 1:27). The Psalmist reflecting on the awesomeness of the human body declared, "... I am fearfully and wonderfully made...(Psalm 139:14). God took on the form of a human body, in Christ, and came and lived among us. Do you need more convincing our body is of great value?

A child enters the world as a helpless baby and his bodily needs for being fed, changed, bathed, clothed and nurtured are totally up to an adult. The mother is usually emotionally and physically tired from the months of pregnancy and labor and delivery. Yet the child has needs and the way in which his needs are met sets an early tone for the child's sense of security. The mom often needs lots of loving support from husband and family in order to care for the needs of the child. Emotionally and physically she is taking care of the baby and dad or someone else is seeing to it that she can focus on that. This is how it should be but unfortunately this is not always true.

While perfection in this area is not possible or required it is important that there be consistency in meeting the baby's physical needs. This helps the child develop the emotional comfort which comes from trusting those who care for him. There will be times when the baby will cry until it is comforted with a bottle or breast but this doesn't hurt the child so long as needs are met on a consistent basis.

Tending to your child's soiled diapers is another way to teach your child his body is important and its functions are acceptable. Your attitude in handling this messy chore needs to indicate no sense of repulsion or disdain for what your child has done. Otherwise, you can set up a sense of shame about his elimination processes which can create unhealthy attitudes about his body.

As your child grows he will become more aware of his body. There is a natural push to grow bigger and to be able to use his body in certain activities. As he is encouraged to become more physically independent and rely on his own skills he develops more confidence in himself and is willing to try new challenges. The overly cautious parent can seriously limit a child in this area and, thus, make him fearful of life.

Several years ago a young boy was brought to me because he was almost paralyzed by his fear of bugs. He didn't want to play outside and, therefore, avoided it whenever possible. Instead he developed a strong attachment to video games he could play with in his room. Since this kept him occupied his parents didn't push the issue until he wanted to join the Scouts. Of course, this meant camping and outside activities when he would encounter bugs and other kinds of critters. Part of my treatment of him was to help him overcome his fear by gradually exposing him to what he feared. When I would take him outside as a part of dealing with his fear he would often want to cling to me until he could adjust to the challenge. He made good progress and was eventually able to deal with being outside without too much stress. What I learned in the process of working with him and his parents was that he had been so protected that he was delayed in many areas of physical accomplishments. At age ten he had not learned to ride a bicycle, was woefully behind in his ability to play games other boys were playing and lacked in confidence and social relationships. This was a clear instance where a child's self esteem had been diminished because he had not been allowed to develop physically because of overprotection and fear.

Another facet of the relationship between our sense of self worth and our physical body is that of personal attractiveness. Our society says beauty is good and not to be beautiful can means you are of less value in our superficial world. We have been so indoctrinated with this value system that we tend to look at children differently based on whether or not they are physically attractive. This narcissistic obsession with physical beauty by a parent can be a real problem for a child. The particularly handsome child can come to attach importance to himself based on his physical attributes. If he doesn't learn to accept these aspects of his physical body as what they are, the result of genetics, he likely will see himself as superior to others or inferior to others based on comparisons. It is always dangerous to build personal value on such external things as beauty since these can change quickly through an illness or accident or over time through the aging process. In a sense the parents of a beautiful or handsome child may face challenges parents of the more ordinary child will not have to deal with, the distraction from the real issue of character or inner beauty.

Children need and deserve total acceptance regardless of their physical abilities or inabilities, attractiveness or unattractiveness. They have been created as persons of worth and have the right to personal respect and dignity.

ACCOMPLISHMENT OR DEFEAT. Here again is a tricky area for parents. And again there is a societal attitude which parents have to deal with . The issue is that winning makes you more valuable than you are if you lose. This is sometimes quite obvious in children's sports activities where parents place more importance on the final score than the effort children make in the game. While I firmly believe children can receive great benefit from competitive sports such as teamwork, individual responsibility and skill development they can also be damaged if the child's sense of worth is attached to whether he wins or loses. Of course, the same can happen related to other areas of accomplishment such as academics, gymnastics, music or any area of accomplishment if the child's sense of value depends on finishing first.

So, what is a wise course of action in this area? It is good to remember we are not all equally endowed but we are all of equal value to God. Some are tall, some are short, some are pretty and some are not so pretty, some are more athletic than others, some are more intelligent than others but all are equally loved by God. We are not to place value on a person on the basis of these kinds of things. We are valuable because God made us in his image and has a purpose for us. When you think of it little children are dependent, can't do much in the way of earning money, don't have a lot of wisdom or know much about the ways of success in the world. In that regard you would have to conclude they are not worth much in a practical sense. Yet Jesus spoke of them this way "…of such is the kingdom of heaven.(Matthew 19:14).

One of the many important truths we can take from the Parable of the Talents (Matthew 25:14-30) is that while we are not given the same gifts we are responsible for the gifts we are given whether great or small. We should help our child discover his gifts, interests and physical abilities and develop all of these for the use and glory of God. We are to do our best with what we have been given. The bottom line goes something like this: our value doesn't depend on what we have been given in comparison to others. Our sense of personal respect is built when we do well with regard to what we have been given, we live up to our capability. When we don't live up to our ability we need to correct the mistake. Thus, through the gradual process of accepting mistakes as a natural way of learning and growing we develop a reasonable and respectful view of our self.

The parent's role in this area is that of coach or mentor to help the child understand and develop abilities . To develop this self- knowledge takes time and patience on the part of the parent and the willingness to allow the child to experiment, make mistakes and discover what is of real interest to him. Perhaps the following ideas will help you think about how to apply these concepts with your child.

Show interest and encouragement in your child's efforts and accomplishments. You may need to train yourself to pay attention to some of things your child needs to accomplish that are ordinary and taken for granted by you. Turning over, sitting up, crawling, walking, running, jumping, talking, singing, putting a puzzle together, tying shoes, buttoning, zipping, using the potty, and learning to skip are all major accomplishments for your child. The list is almost endless if you want to extend it through the middle and teen years. The point is that your child is accomplishing things that are moving him toward physical maturity and the parent who encourages and promotes these accomplishments helps his child feel good because he is growing up.

An important point closely related to this one is the need to encourage the child to do what he can for himself. The parent who insists on doing everything for the child robs him of the opportunity to learn and become confident in himself as a growing person. Your child has an inner push to grow and he needs encouragement in work and play activities that are within his capabilities.

Be realistic about what your child can do. Remember, your child is not an adult in a miniature body. He has physical, emotional, social and intellectual limitations and to expect more than he is capable of doing will frustrate both of you. This is one of the reasons why you need to learn what you can about how children develop and why you need to be a real student in learning about your child. The more you know about him the more compassionate and encouraging you can be with him.

SIGNIFICANT OTHERS. The third and most important factor in the development in your child's sense of value of himself is how significant others, especially you, view him. No one's opinions and attitudes are as important to or influential on your child as those you have about him. Imagine yourself as a large mirror constantly reflecting to your child the attitudes and opinions he should have of himself. To a large degree, this is exactly what is happening on an emotional level between you and your child.

"How would I feel if someone treated me that way?" This may be a good question to use to remind yourself of the powerful effect you have on your child. Your words, slaps, hugs, looks of disgust, surprise or joy reflect the way parents feel about their children at times. Children have an uncanny emotional ability to interpret what you are reflecting to them. What does the mirror say? Are you able to be kind to your child even when you are angry? Or does your child feel he is the reason for your lack of control? Remember, love seeks to do what is in the best interest of your child and the way you deal with your frustrations with him can go a long way in helping him feel positive or negative about himself. While all your experiences with your child will not be positive most of them will be if you keep in mind a few basic issues.

> *The smart parent learns how to give attention and approval.*

I have found in my own experience as a parent and in dealing with hundreds of parents that the parent's attitude and expectations are powerful influences in the child's behavior. Much of the time you get what you expect. If you expect your child to do well and give encouragement and positive guidance you will generally get desirable results. As ridiculous as it may sound, I believe your child wants to please you, to feel that he is doing things that make you proud of him. His bad behavior, the things he does to really irritate you get your attention even if the result for him is some sort of punishment. Your attention is important. So is your approval. The smart parent learns how to give attention and approval. This greatly reduces your child's negative behavior because you are teaching him how to get what he needs by the way he acts. There will be more on this in the chapter on discipline.

Accepting your child unconditionally is a major ingredient in his healthy view of himself. Can he be who he is and be loved without any conditions? This is one of his most important questions in life. He should not have to do anything but be who he is. You give him one of life's greatest blessings when you attach no strings to your love or approval. In my practice I see many adults who are still driven to please a parent whom they felt put conditions on their love. The parent may have died years ago but the person, often very accomplished, is still striving for that elusive sense of total acceptance by the one they wanted most to be proud of them. It's a long, difficult journey for the adult to come to the place to accept the fact that his efforts for approval have not worked. As a parent, you can spare your child from this futile searching for approval through his works by letting him know you accept him unconditionally.

Emphasize the positive in your child's life. Expect and look for ways in which he succeeds and compliment him on his good choices. This is an area in which many well-meaning parents, including myself, make mistakes. We are so concerned about good behavior that we often only see the bad and call attention to it. As a young parent I had to be very aware of this tendency to see the negative more than the positive. "No" was a word I used a great deal until I realized I needed to emphasize what my child was doing well. This didn't mean I would ignore behavior that needed correcting but the shift was one of attitude which led to my change in behavior. This made parenting more pleasant for me and, I'm sure, for my child.

Finally, give them someone to admire and want to emulate. The idea of being a good example to your child may seem to be trite or commonplace but it cannot be overemphasized in the importance of your child's identity and emotional development. You are their first and most powerful image of a man or woman. Your loving, encouraging character can be a lifelong inspiration to them to be the best person they are capable of becoming.

CHAPTER SEVEN

COMMUNICATING
IMPORTANT MESSAGES

Our sense of self and view of life have been deeply influenced by how we have interpreted the events and relationships with significant people in our lives. It was so with our parents and they, in turn, helped shape and color the "lens" through which we view life. And, in turn, we help shape and color the "lens" through which our children view life. And so it has always been. Your words, non-verbal communications and actions send important messages to your child. And your child's positive or negative interpretation of these messages greatly affect how he sees himself and how he approaches life.

Gina's story well illustrates this truth. She is a forty-year-old mother of two children who is divorced. Although she did everything she knew to do to get her husband to love her she never succeeded and felt alone from the beginning of her marriage. He drank too much and she was left to take care of the children while he provided money for the family. When she tried to initiate conversations with him he didn't engage and she felt very lonely. After trying unsuccessfully for twelve years to make the marriage work she decided she was tired of being in a one-way relationship and got a divorce. With the exception that she didn't have to see her former spouse on a daily basis and be reminded of his lack of love for her things did not improve a lot. There was a deeper issue, one that had started with communication from her parents and was duplicated in some ways in her marriage. Her mother was often distracted and silent. Through different ways her father had communicated to her the message that she was not important and not truly loved. As an adult she has struggled with that message about herself, feeling there is something wrong with her. She doubts if anyone is going to love her and if, in fact, God loves her. Her dad's negative actions and the lack of affirming messages by her mom still affect her life today. Since her mother died a few years ago her dad has remarried and has expressed no desire to have a relationship with her and his grandchildren. Her former husband has remarried and goes on with his life seemingly happy and shows no signs of regret for how he treated her. The problem Gina faces now is to reinterpret these important life-messages in light of the truth that her mother, father and former husband were neglectful and uncaring and somehow claim her true identity as a child of God who is loved by him.

Gina's story is a fitting example of how a child's "lens" is developed and influences the interpretation of messages. If your child's "lens" is healthy and she is convinced she is loved and important she can much more easily adjust to your mistakes and forgive you. If the issue of really being loved is in question, as it was for Gina, she will see your mistakes as mounting evidence that you don't really care for her.

By now, it should be abundantly clear that your first job with your child is to help him develop the "lens of love" through which he interprets your messages. You must win his heart because this is his greatest need and will determine to a large degree how he interprets your other communications with him.

Having dealt with the importance of a sense of being loved in the previous chapter and re-emphasizing that fact here we now turn our attention to some of the practical issues of how to communicate those life-altering messages to your child. Communication is a very significant part in all human relationships and learning to communicate well will enhance your ability to create the "lens" through which you want your child to interpret his worth.

Why has God given us the ability to communicate? Communication serves the purpose of transferring information. While there are many modes or methods of communication the essential goal of each is to provide information from one person or party to another. The purposes of communication are varied and may include one or more of the following: to entertain, persuade, inform, deceive, encourage, comfort, propagandize, and educate. Communication is neither good or evil in itself but serves the purpose of the messenger. Each communicator designs his message according to the purpose he wants to accomplish. What are you trying to accomplish in your communication with your child? Is your communication consistent with the goal of providing an environment which encourages your child to grow to be all God intended him to be? If the purpose of life is to love God supremely and to love others as we love our self isn't communication a gift God has given us to accomplish that purpose?

When you communicate well with your child she understands your message the way you intend it. This is true whether you are teaching your child how to make his bed or trying to convey to him deeper issues of the heart such as your affection for him. There are essentially two parts to communication, sending and receiving, and you model both of these for your child.

Sending Messages. Sending messages to your child can be done in many ways. For example, you may put an encouraging note in her backpack for her to discover and read at school. Text messages, e-mails and phone calls are other ways to communicate but are usually one-dimensional and omit the nonverbal aspects which can add so much to communication. Nonverbal ways in which you communicate can be very powerful. You can purposely communicate your approval with a smile or "thumbs up" without saying a word. I've heard numerous persons say all their parent had to do was to give them a certain "look" and whatever they were doing stopped. I have found the "in person" forms of communication can carry a weight others may not because of the combination of spoken words and nonverbal ways of communicating such as touch, voice tone and inflection and facial expressions. Of course, like most anything else, these gifts of communication can be used in a destructive way as well as in a positive and encouraging one.

> *A good rule for parents to follow is to do about twice as much listening as you do talking in conversations with your child.*

Receiving Messages. One of the most important aspects of communication is receiving the message as it is intended. There are two concerns in this process. The first one, to which we've already given some attention, is the way in which the message will be received; the "lens" or willingness to hear by the receiving person. There are times when your child cannot hear because of their anger or hurt and words need to wait until they can be more effective. Or there may be a build up of frustration which has to be worked through before good message sending on your part can be accomplished. This is where the second concern of receiving messages can serve you well. There will be times when you will need to do some fairly intensive listening and less talking in order to help your child begin to listen to you. A good rule for parents to follow is to do about twice as much listening as you do talking in conversations with your child. By this you can understand them better and also teach them the importance of listening, which is the most important skill in communication.

Suggestions for Sending and Receiving Messages

1. Use communication as a tool to build your child's sense of worth. Be very conscious of what you want your child to think about himself and use communication to accomplish your objective. Make a commitment to God to use your words, listening and all other ways of communicating to help your child see himself as a person of worth.

2. Use your personal example to give weight to what you say. Your actions are a major way of communicating with your child. Having integrity between what you say and do actually tells your child he can believe what you say is important. On the other hand, if your personal life is punctuated with dishonesty it will be very difficult for you to teach your child that "honesty is the best policy."

3. Communicate at your child's level of understanding. Develop a pattern which recognizes your child needs you to talk with him in terms he understands. While he will later develop the ability to deal with deeper concepts and words with multiple meanings his early years are limited to concrete and literal thinking. Simplify.

4. Reduce your size. Whenever possible attempt to get down so you can look into your child's eyes as you communicate with him. Getting on your child's eye level reduces the threat of your large size and puts him more at ease in talking to you.

5. Listen with your heart as well as your ears. Effective parents attempt to cultivate the ability to look at life from their child's perspective. Remembering some of your challenges as a child will give you a sense of empathy for the difficulties your child faces being small, unable to use language well and to do many things for himself. Listening with your heart goes beyond hearing words to understanding feelings and concerns which motivate your child. Practicing this will reduce your frustration, deepen your appreciation for your child and help bond you emotionally.

6. Avoid communication traps. Here are a few of the traps which hinder good communication between parent and child.

   (1) Assuming you understand when you really do not. This can happen to any parent because children often have a hard time explaining what they mean. But sometimes it is the fault of the parent who pretends to be listening. This can lead to answering questions your child isn't asking or talking about something totally irrelevant. If you don't understand say so and ask your child to talk further to help you understand. Apologize if you are not listening well and ask your child to tell you again.

   (2) Failure to control your emotions. Sometimes situations are upsetting and your immediate response may be to attack your child rather than calm yourself before dealing with the issue. While anger is an appropriate emotion for some situations it is always wise to be in control of your anger before you deal with your child. Not doing so leads to destructive

communication which hurts your child. A habit of this lack of control will eventually damage communication and work against your goal of helping your child see himself as a person of worth.

(3) Sending double messages. A double message takes place when the emotional tone or body language is different from the words spoken. For example, if your child asks if you are angry with him tell him the truth because your body language is already communicating something to him. Be aware of your feelings and work at being honest with them so that you do not confuse your child by words that betray the truth. Being cheerful and happy all the time does not guarantee your child will be emotionally healthy. If you will deal with your feelings in a healthy way you will avoid this communication trap while teaching your child how to express his feelings in a healthy way.

(4) Assuming silence is bad. Sometimes a smile, look or touch can say more than a thousand words. One of the pitfalls I faced in rearing my children was the temptation to talk too much. Perhaps you also overdose your child with so many words that your words seem to loose significance. Words can carry great weight if we use them wisely and do not assume we must be talking all the time. There are times when silence is indeed golden.

(5) Assuming listening is for children and talking is for adults. This is perhaps the most common false assumption parents make

when communicating with their child. They want to be sure their child listens to them but they do not listen to their child. Parents who know their children at a deep level have learned to listen to them. Understanding your child's heart is a key to providing the kind of environment in which he can thrive. Listen, listen, listen.

CHAPTER EIGHT

WORKING YOURSELF
OUT OF A JOB

The parents were quite distressed when they came to see me. Their son, George, was twenty years old, wouldn't keep a job and still living at home. They wanted to know what I would recommend they do about George. My initial feeling was they should kick him out and force him to learn some facts about life but I thought better of it and suggested he be sent to see me so I could assess the situation before any course of action was taken. George's mild depression was caused primarily by the fact that his laziness and approach to life were not working for him. Dad had begun putting some pressure on him to get a job and pay for his car insurance and help out with living expenses. To deal with this pressure to grow up George would get a job but do something to sabotage it and lose the job in a couple of weeks. He did this several times but each time would blame the boss or a co-worker for his plight in life. At one point his mom got so fed up with him that she demanded he get a job or find another place to live. He dealt with this by pretending to have a job. He got up and got ready as if going to work but instead would drive around, go to a park or do something to take up the required time and return home. When I asked him what he would do if his mom required proof of his employment or money he had no answer. George was stuck, an eight-year-old in a twenty-year-old body. At the time when he should be launching himself into independence from his parents he was not ready for the real world. He was still dependent, emotionally, physically and financially.

George's situation was really sad. His only options at this point seemed to be to remain dependent on his parents or some agency or to be put out on his own to grow up the hard way. His parents were certainly culpable in his failure to grow up and were now, many years late, trying to address the issue. They had failed to work themselves out of a job. They were still trying to parent a twenty-year-old. If they had dealt with George as he needed when the opportunities presented themselves naturally they would have spared themselves and George lots of heartache and misery.

As a parent you need to consider what happened to George and his parents so this kind of thing doesn't happen to you and your child. Be very conscious of the fact that you must do your best to prepare your child to be on his own, to become independent of you and develop his own life. God has meant life to be this way and it is a lack of real love and understanding when a child becomes so dependent on a parent that they cannot emotionally function on their own.

So, how do you work yourself out of a job as a parent? Obviously, it is not by waiting to address the issue when you are forced to do so. No, it is a slow, gradual process that balances your child's real dependency needs with their ability to safely assume increasing amounts of independence. To see how this process works we will need to look at dependence, independence and interdependence to discover what is involved in each and how they relate to each other.

Dependence. As stated earlier, a child comes into the world totally dependent. For a while you must do everything for him so that his physical needs are met. As you do this in a caring way your child develops a sense of trust in you and relaxes in the security of your care. In God's plan for your child there are progressive stages of physical development such as turning over, sitting up, scooting, crawling, walking, and talking. As your child is going through the physical development process he is going to want to attempt to do things for himself such as washing his hair, brushing his teeth, buttoning, zipping, and other tasks which show he is growing up. You may often hear "Me do it" as a way of telling you he wants to try. This is as it should be because he wants to grow and be big like you.

Keeping a child physically dependent when he is ready to do things for himself not only stifles his development of physical skills but also hurts his sense of self by denying him the joy of accomplishment. Of course there are times you must protect your child from attempting things that may seriously injure him but being overprotective can create a fear that causes him to not attempt tasks well within his ability.

Dependence upon a caring parent is a wonderful thing for a child because it means what the child cannot do for himself the parent will do. This produces trust and a sense of well-being which really allows your child to want to grow and become less dependent on you as he matures.

The problem in dependence for the child comes when the parent is so fearful or possessive that she limits the child's growth by continuing to do for him what he can do for himself. Her emotional need can cripple the child. This happens when the child becomes the parent's focus of love in an unhappy marriage. The child is substituted for the husband or wife and is "spoiled" in an attempt by the parent to meet an unfulfilled emotional need in the marriage. Or this type "spoiling" can happen when a parent tries to make up for what he didn't have growing up by giving everything to his child. The following story illustrates how this can happen.

At fifty Andrew is just now beginning to grow up. While he was supposed to be growing up his father provided all the things he had wanted for himself and refused to let Andrew take a job or make his own way in anything. In college he was provided a nice car, all the money he needed and was discouraged from becoming financially less dependent. He left college before graduating to pursue a career as a musician. He was lost in life without a plan and no sense of direction. Andrew continued to accept money from his father for several years and into the early years of marriage until his wife would have no more of it. Ten years after leaving college he went back to complete his degree. However, he has never had a job in which he earned a substantial living and now works at a minimum wage job. In looking back on the last three decades Andrew laments the fact that he allowed himself to be so lazy and remain dependent on his dad. This early pattern persisted through his young adult years and now Andrew, at fifty, is having to attempt to repair damages his lack of responsibility has done to his family and to himself.

Andrew's dad is not responsible for Andrew's adult decisions and the results of those choices. However, it is unmistakable that his own frustrations with life and unfulfilled dreams led him to take actions which influenced Andrew to take the path of least resistance and remain dependent. What child growing up could resist such a temptation?

Independence. Adult life, being grown up, calls for a sense of independence. For example, when we marry it is important that we "leave and cleave." (Ephesians 5:31). The new couple is to put each other above all other human relationships. This is extremely difficult and troublesome when one of them is too dependent on a parent or someone else to leave emotionally. It is also financially irresponsible for parents to continue to support the couple, as in Andrew's case, except in emergencies. There should be the expectation placed on children that when they reach young adulthood they are on their own. If your child is mature enough to get married he is mature enough to assume financial responsibility for his life. There is no single right way to handle this but you need to set the stage for these events early in life by gradually preparing your child to take over your responsibility for him.

I think of this growing in independence as a process very much like teaching your child how to ride a bicycle. If you have attempted to teach your child to ride a bike you know it is a matter of knowing when to hold on and when to turn loose. This was the case when I was teaching Kristen, then six, how to ride. I had had some previous training at this by helping Nathan but I had to work individually with her just as I had with Nathan. My job was essentially to know when she needed me and when she didn't without letting my fear get in the way.

This is how the process went. I held the bike steady while she got on and continued to balance it for her while she made the necessary adjustments. She got herself comfortably seated, positioned her feet on the peddles and brushed her hair out of her eyes. I continued to wait patiently and balance the bike as she took a few deep breaths and gathered her courage. Then the big moment came and she said "GO." Her legs and feet started moving and the wheels began turning. I stayed beside her, walking quickly, still supporting her until she could balance herself on the bike. As we picked up speed she gave the signal, "Let go." With a mixture of pride and fear I turned loose and she was on her own. I continued to run beside her just in case she needed me, encouraging her effort and progress. Then I stopped and allowed her to finish the ride by herself and waited for her to return to me. As she neared the end of the ride a big smile crossed her face and she signaled me again, "Okay, Dad, stop me." It was time for me to hold on again.

As Kristen practiced learning to ride her bike I found I was doing less holding on and more letting go until she was completely on her own. She had moved from dependence to independence in this task and needed my help no more. I had worked myself out of this job and the newfound skill brought great pleasure and confidence to Kristen for many years. And as she continued to grow and mature there were many more ways in which her mom and I would alternately hold on and turn loose in order to help her grow toward the wonderful young wife and mother she is today.

Here are some ideas you may want to consider in the process of helping your child move from dependence to independence:

Utilize your child's desire to be big. Most young children want to do things they see big people do. They don't view these things as work. Start at an early age inviting your child to do simple tasks they can do. For example, when a young child can rub his head he can be taught to help wash his hair. When he can pick up toys he can also pick them up to put them away. Get the idea?

Take cues from your child. He may tell you directly when he wants to do something with a "Me do it" or he may attempt to do something on his own. Allow him to try and help him only where necessary. This applies to older children as well. Where possible allow them to help when they show interest.

1. Allow your child to do what he can for himself. This is a major concept in teaching a child to become more self-reliant. Of course, allowing your child to do things for himself takes more time but the long term benefit will be much better. Children detest being "mothered" too much when they can handle a task on their own.

2. Increase your child's freedom and responsibility as he is ready. As your child becomes consistent in handling

certain tasks you can then expand his freedom and responsibility in that area. For example, when your child learns to tell time you can give him the freedom and responsibility to come home at a given time without you having to call and remind him. Be careful not to overload your child with freedom or responsibility since the main goal is to see him succeed and become more independent. Should he fail in an assignment you may need to consider talking with him to see if an adjustment is needed.

3. Give your child specific tasks and hold him accountable for those tasks. Start early to teach your child to help with making his bed, folding and putting away his clothes, and other small tasks and expect him to do it. While a child's life shouldn't be dominated by work it is important to help him begin to see that being part of your family means learning to work together. There are many household chores such as learning to use the washer, unloading the dishwasher, vacuuming and emptying trash cans which take little time and teach your child to become more independent. Their future spouse will praise you for teaching them how to do practical things around the house. If your child remains single they will need to be able to do all these things anyway. Either way you and your child both win.

Interdependence. Interdependence involves a voluntary and healthy dependence on each other such as that between a husband and wife or a family where members rely on each other to make the family functional. The process of helping your child move from dependence to independence will also bring about interdependence, an indispensable quality of healthy relationships. As your child develops a healthy sense of independence he will not only learn to think of himself but of the needs of others. He will learn to cooperate with family rules and work for the good of the family and not just consider his own needs. He will maintain his individuality and personal boundaries but will be able to choose to be interdependent with others. In a functional family a child will be able to grow up and leave without guilt and with the blessing of parents.

Since your task is to work yourself out of a job it is good that you realize how important this process of dependence, independence and interdependence really is. Done well it prepares your child for a life of emotional, social, physical, and spiritual independence from you. Done well it also gives your child the basis for further developing interdependence with a mate and enjoying a functional family relationship. After years of seeing all kinds of marriage issues I am convinced that a good marriage is made up of two independent people who have committed to be interdependent. You can influence your child's future family and your grandchildren by beginning to work yourself out of a job while your child is very young.

CHAPTER NINE

ENCOURAGING SELF-DISCIPLINE

Jonnie is a well-adjusted mom of four who is able to deal with the stresses of everyday life without falling apart when unexpected calamities occur or life throws her a curve. When her Dad died last year she experienced a deep loss. As she continued her grieving process she sought some professional help to address issues she didn't know how to deal with. While this loss has definitely affected her she has been able to go on with life. Much of her ability to deal with her loss in such a positive way she attributes to the self-discipline she developed in growing up in her home. This self-discipline has not only helped her grow through the pain of the greatest loss she has yet experienced in life but has benefited her in her personal health routines and in taking care of an active family.

> *one of the most telling signs of maturity is to be able to deal with reality in a way which leads to functional living.*

In my opinion one of the most telling signs of maturity is to be able to deal with reality in a way which leads to functional living. This growth in self-discipline can happen in spite of parental influences to the contrary but the easier path is to grow up with parents who disciplined you well.

> *Healthy love seeks to influence character development which results in behavior which blesses the child and those around him.*

Love is doing what is in your child's best interest. Love takes the long view and considers what will be the end result when a certain course of training is practiced. Children are trained to know what is acceptable behavior by default, by example or by deliberate or intentional teaching. Healthy love seeks to influence character development which results in behavior which blesses the child and those around him. Children who develop good character are loved well and are disciplined well.

Self-control or self-discipline is the rare personal characteristic of a person who has truly taken responsibility for himself. Such a person has internalized an external discipline which has brought him to own his feelings, thoughts, words and actions, a rather unusual quality in today's fast-paced, quick-fix culture.

> *Good discipline is teaching about and encouraging good behavior as well as discouraging bad behavior.*

While you cannot give your child the gift of self-discipline you can encourage this valuable trait through an approach toward discipline which, if followed by your child, will bring about an internalization of values which will benefit him his entire life. It is my purpose here to identify some of the major issues of discipline and discuss principles which will put you on a good path toward helping your child become a self-disciplined person.

What is good discipline? Many people tend to think of spanking or a verbal reprimand to correct bad behavior as "discipline." This is unfortunate because it is much too narrow a view of the issue. Good discipline is more than stopping bad behavior. Good discipline is teaching about and encouraging good behavior as well as discouraging bad behavior. Seeing discipline as punishment only can be dangerous because this view tends to deal with bad behavior and ignore good behavior. This can teach your child the only successful way to get attention is through bad behavior.

> *Discipline is a process of teaching your child how he should act in such a manner that he can gradually internalize your teaching and incorporate your expectations into the way he behaves.*

Discipline is a process of teaching your child how he should act in such a manner that he can gradually internalize your teaching and incorporate your expectations into the way he behaves.

Think about this idea of discipline. What is it really about?

Discipline is a process of teaching. Children need to be taught how to behave, what is acceptable and what is not. Good teachers have a plan, an idea of what they want their student to learn in order to succeed in that area of knowledge. What is your plan or wish for your child? What kind of character do you want him to have? What kind of values do you want him to live by? How do you want him to treat himself, others and God? Discipline is the process of teaching your child the foundational ideas and values which will shape his behavior.

Discipline is a "process." Process involves gradual movement toward a goal. It involves one step which leads to the next and on to the next until the end is reached. For example, imagine the process of disciplining your child like that of climbing a flight of stairs. The goal is to get to the next floor but to reach the goal you must go through the process of walking up each step until you have reached the top. So it is with discipline. There is no elevator or escalator, no quick way to teach your child how to become self-disciplined. Obviously, helping your child learn discipline requires patience and persistence on your part. It involves courage and clarity of purpose and the willingness to forgive yourself when you mess up and the will to discipline yourself to correct your mistakes.

Most of your discipline of your child will take place in an informal setting such as your house, the market or on a trip to your relatives. You will gradually teach your child through daily activities such as changing diapers, feeding, playing, taking a bath, getting ready for bedtime, school assignments, play activities, playing with friends, watching TV together and hundreds of other ways in which you interact with him. You will be in this process of discipline from the time your child is born until he assumes full responsibility for himself.

Discipline involves expectations. Good discipline involves a long range view of what kind of person you want your young child to grow up to be. For the Christian parent these expectations should be a result of the understanding of the meaning of life and the teachings of Scripture regarding personal character. They involve such ideals as love for self, others and God. Reverence for life, honesty, humility, compassion, industry, generosity, patience, endurance and humility are examples of expectations you would probably add to your list. These kinds of ideals are the goal, the ultimate expectation for your child. As you know from your personal struggles in some of these areas you cannot expect a young child to quickly incorporate these values into his life. But in the process of life with you, you will gradually guide him toward these character traits. Please be patient and cautious with your child at this point not to expect him to act beyond his level of maturity. For example, most parents want their child to be unselfish and share their toys with others, an admirable goal. Remember however, this is a process and to force a two-year old to relinquish his toy to another is unfair to him. Recognize the fact that he cannot do this emotionally until he is secure in the fact that the toy is his and he can willingly share it. Work with your child where he is and gradually help him to learn to share and take turns. Give him time, respect his feelings and gradually guide him to grow toward your goal. This way, he can begin to internalize the behavior rather than feeling forced to behave. This is an important concept in discipline and worth remembering. Whenever possible attempt to gain your child's cooperation rather than just ignoring his will. Certainly there are times when you need to take control of things but if your major approach is to work with your child to gain their cooperation you will find the discipline process much easier for both of you.

Your role in discipline involves several important functions. For example, you are responsible for deciding the values and behaviors you want your child to learn. In a real sense you are actually your child's first "god" because you are determining by choice or default the way you will rear you child. You exert an authority in your child's life to bless or curse him by your choices. Serious business isn't it?

Another aspect of your role in discipline is enforcement of your expectations. Without enforcement your ideals and words will produce nothing but confusion and frustration. Many children, perhaps yours, will test to see if you really mean what you say. They don't really understand you want them to act in certain ways because it will benefit them later. They're not interested in later. They are interested in what they want now. It is your role to encourage acceptable behavior and discourage unacceptable behavior by enforcing your expectations with consistent and encouraging guidance and,

Parenting With a Purpose

when necessary, punishment which effectively addresses the wrong behavior.

Good discipline uses an encouraging manner. The "manner" you use with your child may be one of the most over-looked but important factors in discipline. Good discipline is not just about having and enforcing expectations but "how" you go about doing that. Two words you will want to remember in your discipline with your child are FRIENDLY and FIRM. Be friendly and firm with your child when you are having to correct a situation. For example, saying in a firm and friendly tone, " Johnny, please don't climb on the chair. You must play on the floor," can communicate what is and is not acceptable to you. If Johnny decides not to listen to you then put him on the floor and continue to reinforce your point. Of course, this situation could be handled in a destructive way by yelling at him or jerking him from the chair. The key to positive discipline is a loving, firm manner. Be firm, yet loving. You do not have to hurt your child by being physically rough with him. You can speak to him or restrain him without abusing his character. Your tone of voice can indicate your firmness without implying you dislike him.

Be firm, yet loving.

One of your goals in using a friendly and firm manner in correcting your child's behavior is to help him realize you love him and what you require of him is for his good. Otherwise, you run the risk of your child concluding that your correction is because you don't like him. Your child may show his immaturity and protest your decision and declare how mean he thinks you are. But remember he is a child and, deep down, he is comforted to know that you are in charge and he has you to care for him.

Good discipline brings change. Children who are disciplined by love often choose to follow behaviors taught by their parents. This internalization of values begins in the preschool years, continues in childhood and youth and is refined and "owned" as the maturing process continues. Hopefully, by the time your child is on his own you will be able to turn him loose with the confidence that he has the basic tools to not only survive the challenges of life but to make a positive difference. The ultimate goal of your discipline is your child's self-discipline. When he holds himself accountable for his life and orders his choices by an internal set of values which honor himself, God and others what you have worked for is in place. His life will be blessed and he will bless others. And, your child at some point will recognize the great debt of gratitude he owes you for the love which brought such good discipline to his life.

> *The ultimate goal of your discipline is your child's self-discipline.*

Ten Principles of Discipline

You can use the following principles or essential elements of discipline to determine how you will go about providing guidance for your child. These principles are solid, time-tested concepts which, if applied consistently, will greatly help you in this vitally important parenting task.

1. **The parent is the authority in the home.** This is how God intended it and you, the parent, must take and use this responsibility wisely. Your child is not to be in charge of deciding what is best for himself. He is not equipped intellectually, socially or emotionally to do so. I personally believe it is a good practice to discuss situations and explain decisions with your child so he can understand your process and that he has been heard. I also believe children should be allowed to express their opinions, concerns and disagreements but the final decision and responsibility rests on the parent.

2. **Parents should be united.** Parents who are in open conflict about how to handle consequences of misbehavior or how to handle other discipline issues create confusion for their child. This usually results from the unwillingness or inability to communicate about these issues on a regular basis. If this is not addressed properly the child may try to divide the parents in order to get what he wants. When this happens you have an unhealthy alignment of power of a child and parent against the other parent. This is too much power for a child and will continue to deteriorate the marriage. The child's place is to be under the authority of the parents and parents have the responsibility to be united in the wise use of that authority. To use their responsibility well both parents need to agree to support each other and discuss their differences out of the presence of the child. They should also anticipate their child's actions and think together about how they will handle issues as they arise. So, some talking about "what if?" will help keep you a step ahead of your child and keep you united on how to guide your child.

3. **Every child is unique.** The child God gave you is like no other. Although he has the same basic needs and similar characteristics as other children he doesn't have the same personality or process all things the same way as other children. If you have more than one child you have discovered your children may be very different in temperament and personality. You cannot work with both children the exact same way and get the desired results. This is especially true in methods you use in discipline, especially in correcting behavior. Some parents mistakenly believe spanking is the solution to all problems. While this form of punishment may help when there is a direct defiance

of your authority it is not a good solution for most routine issues. Some children are not helped by spanking and some respond better to other methods such as talking to them or times-out.

The issue is to know your child and what works best for him. Playing with your him, observing and evaluating his moods and behavior will help you do a good job your discipline to his needs. This is the idea behind the Proverb writer's words in Proverbs 22:6, "Train a child in the way he should go, and when he is old he will not turn from it." This approach is often uncomfortable because it recognizes the need for the parent to be flexible, to think and grow as the child changes.

4. **All behavior has a cause.** One of the most important aspects in guiding your child's behavior is to attempt to understand why he acts as he does. Sometimes unacceptable behavior is stopped quickly by understanding what circumstances influenced the behavior. For example, you may discover that your inadvertent delay in feeding your child has triggered his outrage. Your child acts out of needs. Hunger, sleepiness, over-stimulation, lack of attention or a number of other things may be behind his acting out. Conversely, the same is true for your child's acceptable behavior. So, it is a good idea to search for the why in all your child's behavior because all his behavior has an underlying cause. "Why does he do that?" is an important question and one which should lead you to investigate reasons behind your child's behavior.

5. **A child tends to repeat behavior for which he is rewarded.** This is true whether the behavior being rewarded is good or bad. What will your child do

if you laugh at his behavior? Most likely he will do what he did again. When he is young your child doesn't choose to behave a certain way on the basis of whether or not he thinks the action is right or wrong. His choice is to do what gets rewarded. Since this principle is true why not think of reinforcing good behaviors with compliments, a smile or pat on the back.

6. **A child tends to stop behavior for which he is not rewarded.** Sometimes simply ignoring some behaviors will stop them because your child is not getting your attention. Sometimes telling your child to stop the behavior or redirecting it will get the results you want. At other times an appropriate punishment is necessary to show your child the action will not be tolerated. In either instance your child does not get what he wants and begins to realize this behavior doesn't work.

7. **Good discipline accentuates the positive.** Expect your child to do well, to obey and you may be surprised at how your attitude will influence his behavior. Look for ways to say and do affirming things and you will set a positive expectation for your child. Let go of the burden of being a behavior policeman who is always looking for bad behavior to correct. Expect the good and you will find lots of joy in the discipline process with your child. All children misbehave at times or they wouldn't be human but, in general, I have found that parents usually get the behavior they expect from their child.

8. **Punishment should be appropriate and come as soon as possible after the offense.** Sometimes the punishment is to do what would seem a natural consequence of the behavior. I once instructed a

parent to charge her child for the time it cost her to go back to school and get a book he forgot. So, he paid her back for the thirty minutes by pulling weeds for thirty minutes in the flower bed. No more forgotten books. Another part of this principle is the need to connect the punishment to the behavior as soon as possible so the child, especially if he is young, will see the relationship to his unacceptable behavior. For example, if your child misuses a toy he will lose immediate use of that toy. The immediate consequence helps the young child connect it to what he did. For a young child, waiting a few minutes to correct behavior will undo the connection between the action and the punishment.

9. **Use your child's two major forces to guide behavior.** God made your child with two strong forces which you can use to guide him. First, your child wants to please you and be approved by you. This may sound ridiculous but it is true. Let your child know what pleases you and when he pleases you. Compliment him and do not withhold encouragement. Second, your child wants to grow up, to be big like you. Allow your child to do things to help you and compliment him for it. For example, saying something like "Maggie, thank you, for putting the napkins on the table. You are getting to be a big girl." can do wonders for a child's behavior.

10. **Good discipline is consistent.** One of the most difficult but important aspects of the discipline process is to become consistent. Children establish good behavior habits when parents are consistent in the way they deal with them. So, your discipline must be disciplined. Inconsistency is confusing and ineffective because it gives the message that the expected behavior

is not important all the time. Consistency has two important parts. First, there needs to be consistency in the sense that the behavior is dealt with the same way each time it occurs. Second, parents need to be consistent in the way the action is dealt with. This goes back to need for parents to be united in how behavior is handled. When one parent handles the issues the same as the other the child soon gets the idea of what to expect and this helps him consider the consequences of his actions.

CONCLUSION

Parenting is difficult work. It is often more difficult than it has to be because it lacks real direction. Without a guiding purpose the pieces don't interlock and work together as they should.

Without a sense of purpose and strategies to make the purpose work it is easy to become discouraged and wonder if what you are doing is helping to influence your child in a positive way.

Hopefully, after reading Parenting With A Purpose you have a clear understanding of your purpose as a parent and some definite ideas to give your child a great opportunity to become successful in what matters most in life, relationships. It is my hope and prayer that I have communicated the important ideas of this book in a way which will encourage you to read it time and again until the major concepts become deeply imbedded in your heart and mind. If you apply the teachings of this book it is my strong belief that you and your child and potentially future generations will be blessed by its truth.

Please remember, effective parenting begins with your character. Who you are really matters. Therefore, I want to leave you with a challenge. As a beginning step in your growing commitment as a parent, write a brief description of the kind of person you want God to help you work on becoming. As a reminder of your desire to grow as a person put the statement in your Bible or some other place where you will see it often.

Mother

    With God's help I want to _____

_____

_____

    Date   Signed

Father

    With God's help I want to _____

_____

_____

_____

    Date   Signed